THE NO GARLIC COOKBOOK
Italian Classics

D1826947

This edition first published in August 2018

Copyright © Keith Chamberlain

All rights reserved. No part of this publication may be reproduced in any material form (including scanning, photocopying or storing in any medium by electronic means and whether or not transiently or incidentally to some other use of this publication) without the copyright owner's written permission, except in accordance with the provisions of the Copyright, Designs and Patents Act 1988 or under the terms of a license issued by the copyright Licensing agency, 90 Tottenham Court Road, London, W1P 9HE. Applications for the copyright owner's permission to reproduce any part of this publication should be addressed to the publisher.

The moral right of the author has been asserted in accordance with the Copyright, Designs and Patents Act 1988.

Printed and bound in the UK

ISBN: 978-1-9995948-4-8

A CIP catalogue record for this book is available from the British library.

This book can be ordered direct from the publishers at:

www.greentechpublishing.com

ACKNOWLEDGEMENTS

I would like to thank all the people who have acted as guinea pigs and consumed my delicious NON-GARLIC food over the years at all the fabulous parties that I have been honoured to host and serve. Special thanks must also go to the many great Italian chefs whose garlic free cooking was the catalyst for this second book in the NO GARLIC series. It was their cooking and presentation skills whilst I was working in Italy and my love of cooking over the years that motivated me to compile this book, the idea and inspiration of which has been sitting on the shelf for more than 10 years.

Finally, thanks go to the team at Greentech publishing, who have provided the perfect balance of critical feedback and support, especially Nick who has once again used his artistic skills to create a great cover and interior design leading up to this second volume, in what is an ongoing series of NO GARLIC scrumptiously gastronomic cookbooks.

To Hannah and Maisie.

CONTENTS

 = SUITABLE FOR VEGETARIANS

BEEF

VEAL

CHICKEN

PESCE (Fish)

VEGETARIANO

THE NO GARLIC COOKBOOK
Italian Classics

WELCOME

This book is the culmination of 20 years' experience perfecting and cooking freshly made garlic free meals. After working in Italy, I took traditional recipes, many with not a hint of garlic in sight. Then, after discovering that there is growing trend toward garlic free cooking thoughout this great country, it inspired me to compile a collection of my favourite Italian classics, previously only handwritten by me in note form.

I have purposely chosen a selection of my take on the most flavoursome, mouth-watering Italian dishes; all garlic free, and none the worse for its absence. All recipes have been tried, tweaked and tested at numerous events over the past 20 years or more. The trend to cook GARLIC FREE in Italy is to be commended and at last brings out all the delicious flavours from each of my recipe's fresh ingredients.

Like me, many of you reading this book will have very busy lifestyles and so I have made the recipes as simple to prepare and cook as possible. If the recipe asks for chopped tomato, you can either skin and chop fresh Italian bell tomatoes or source a non-garlic jar or tin from your local supermarket, rather than make your own. Although, making your own pizza dough is a must. But generally, almost all of the ingredients are fresh and readily available in your local stores.

This is the second volume of No Garlic cookbooks, packed with recipes that have been fine-tuned over the years for people who, like me, have constantly been on the lookout for garlic-free food that's both healthy, nutritious and delicious. You'll be surprised by what you're able to achieve. In all recipes, the NO GARLIC methods taste far superior than the garlic-based alternatives. I want to show you how you can eat the most delicious meals without a hint of garlic. All my recipes are incredibly satisfying and easy to cook.

It's a new way of cooking for most. The use of garlic in everyday meals is now so ingrained in our diet that even snacks like crisps can contain the dreaded G word. But to return to the concept of garlic free cooking, we have to go back to the 1960s, when the vast majority of meals were traditionally cooked with fresh wholesome ingredients and traditional spices and herbs.

I promise that you will find this book inspiring, to the extent that you will want to invite your friends and family around to taste your new full flavour garlic-free food, the way it used to be and the way it is now in most parts of Italy and the majority of Japan, as the tide is finally turning against garlic. So, whether you have an intolerance or an allergic reaction to garlic, or you just want to go odour and garlic-breath free from now on or are simply inquisitive to know how great it could possibly be to eat garlic free. Then this book is for you.

INTRODUCTION

My relationship with food has always been a pleasant and rewarding experience, but garlic has been an unwelcome foe for as long as I can remember. I grew up in the cobbled terraces of inner Birmingham and every evening would retch and heave at the potent smell of garlic drifting from my neighbours' backyards at teatime. I didn't know then, but it was clearly my body warning me that this smell was not good for me. It was a form of bodily alarm.

In the sixties, garlic was not a mainstream ingredient in the typical British meal. The country was really only just getting over rationing from the war years and easy traditional meals tended to be the norm, made with what ingredients were available at the time. Thus, meals such as Sunday roast, fish and chips, bangers and mash, toad in the hole, and beans and cheese on toast, seemed to be the standard by which a growing family was nourished. Dessert was usually tinned sliced peaches with evaporated milk and a few slices of thin white bread and butter for afters. Apparently, bread and butter with dessert was a cheap way to fill hungry stomachs for the rest of the day.

Being a full-time stay at home mother looking after 4 children, my mother's life was never easy. No washing machine, no fridge, no spin drier, no bathoom, just an outside toilet. Unfortunately for my Dad, brothers, sister and I, mums cooking was, to be blunt, below par. This was the catalyst that spurred me to develop my own cooking skills from an early age and is why I looked forward to school dinners so much.

Then about 15 years ago, I took a business colleague for lunch to a French Bistro. I remember vividly that the first course was pea and ham soup. Literally seconds after the first spoonful, I was told that my lips turned blue, I had difficulty breathing and then minutes later, stomach cramps commenced. This was the last time that I have knowingly eaten garlic and now make a point of thoroughly checking menus with waiters and chefs when eating out. Because of this problem, I can't eat processed food. Even snacks like crisps have the dreaded G in them. The upside is that all the food I eat, is prepared and cooked fresh, creating flavoursome culinary delights for all who eat with me.

THE HISTORY OF GARLIC

The plant, garlic, originated from Asia and is from the onion genus species. Its close family are chives, shallots, leeks and onions. It has been used by humans for many years for both medicinal and culinary purposes. Often used as a pungent flavour for spicy dishes. It is much paraded for its alleged super food traits and supposed health benefits. It has gained an almost cult like following amongst the likes of raw food fans, vegans and vegetarians. There have been many claims over the years that consumption can lower blood pressure, lower cholesterol and has antibacterial characteristics too. It has also been long known that some gardeners use it as a very effective organic pesticide, by placing it next to plants that need protection against pests or as a liquid spray. Due to the allicin chemical in each bulb, it is worth noting that there is no known animal that will eat this pungent vegetable. Of course, its taste and odour are enough to repel any potential predators, including vampires!

IS GARLIC A POISON?

Doctors recommend that pregnant women, especially those that intend to breastfeed, should avoid garlic completely as it has been linked to miscarriages as well as altering the behavioural patterns of infants (2). This alone should make one question its worth and safety for human consumption.

Garlic is a rubefacient matter and when directly applied to the skins surface in oil form, it will cause redness, swelling and often inflammation (1). This is the result of the immune system attempting to isolate the garlic so that it does no further harm to the body.

None the less, there are some assumed health benefits such as the ability to lower blood pressure (4) and its ability to lower cholesterol (3). It has been known for centuries that garlic is an anti-bacterial food that can totally destroy all bacteria, good and bad. Few people believe that that is a good thing though. Of course, most people want something that can kill off germs, but there can be destructive effects, worse even than having a bacterial infection, due to its non-discriminatory characteristics. This is why I personally would not advocate consumption of garlic and there are even more reasons. Some studies have shown that garlic can cause damage to brain cells, due to its very powerful effect of entering the bloodstream, especially if eaten in raw form. Although, when cooked, the toxic or negative effect of garlic is greatly reduced.

Garlic can also burn. According to several sources, It has the ability to burn tiny holes though the lining of the intestines (2). This can be particularly bad for sufferers of IBS for instance. It can penetrate the mucus lining and proceed into the intestinal wall, burning tiny holes that can eventually lead to perforations and ultimately the garlic can then enter the bloodstream.

World War 2 veterans, especially those of Italian descent, were extremely knowledgeable about the toxic effects of garlic. If you feed a dog raw garlic, you can kill it. Apparently, some frontline soldiers stocked up with garlic bulbs and after squashing a clove, covered the garlic fluid over their bullets and loaded their weapons. Anecdotal reports suggested that despite some pretty poor marksmen, the garlic laden bullets gave them an advantage when it came to killing their foe. The frontline Italian soldiers knew that once garlic entered the bloodstream, the enemy would die, wherever they hit them.

THE TIDE IS TURNING

Completely unrelated to the Italians wartime military tactics, there is a whole new movement in Italy that is moving away from adding garlic to food, especially when using fresh ingredients. There are many self-publicised 'garlic-free' restaurants appearing all over the country. A new renaissance where all the great chefs are learning to cook without garlic. I am very familiar with Milan, having worked there a few years ago. Even then, the vast majority of eateries in this great Italian city, cooked garlic-free.

Interestingly, garlic only became popular in southern Mediterranean countries when there was a shortage of food and no fresh herbs or spices were available. This was particularly evident during war times. As poverty increased, fragrant spices were substituted for cheaper, widely available garlic to give their food some flavour. This trend spread thoughout the world during the major conflicts of the last centuries due to fresh food and spice shortages, affecting mainly the poor communities of each country. The trend of garlic reversal and eradication in Italy, will hopefully spread further afield.

It's no secret that a country, recognised as having some of the oldest residents in the world, has an almost completely garlic-free diet. The Japanese are very proud of their culinary traditions and they remain the only country in the world to gain UNESCO cultural heritage status for their food. It's no coincidence then that garlic is not a staple ingredient in any Japanese traditional food.

The recipe for Bolognese sauce in Bologna is fiercely protected by the local chamber of commerce and calls for absolutely no garlic in the recipe.

Even the famous late great Italian chef, Marcella Hazan, insisted on no garlic in her tomato-based dishes. She once said, 'the single greatest cause of failure in would-be Italian cooking, was the unbalanced use of garlic'.

The 'no garlic' trend of restaurants is slowly but surely evolving in the UK. I have a local restaurant that almost exclusively cooks the entire menu garlic free. Long may it continue. I long to see the day when the pungent, overpowering, foul smelling bulb, is eradicated from our shores.

In other words, the reason that there is an ensuing revolt against the use of garlic amongst some of the world's top chefs, is as Hazan puts it," real recipes don't lean on garlic as a crutch, because their ingredients taste better to begin with, they possess true flavour" ...Let the flavour commence!

BIBLIOGRAPHY

1. Baruchin AM et al. 2001. Garlic Burns p781-782.
2. Barnes J Anderson, Philipson JD. Herbal medicines. Pharmaceutical press, London. 2012.
3. Murray MT. The healing power of herbs. London. 4th edition. Original 1995.
4. Ackerman RT et al. Garlic shows promise for some cardo vascular risk factors. Arch intern Med. 2001:161: 813-824.

"

If your mother cooks Italian food, why should you go to a restaurant?

"

--- MARTIN SCORSESE

IL PRIMO

(FIRST MEAL OR STARTER)

Magnificent MOZZARELLA & FRESH HERB CHEESE BALLS

Serves	6
Prep time	10m
Marination	4h
Total time	4h 10m

Marinated baby mozzarella balls are really popular. You can freely buy these super mini cheese balls at your local supermarket, but at a cost. If you have time, its best to make your own marinated mozzarella balls.

The mozzarella balls are marinated in fresh herbs, olive oil, salt and lemon juice. You will need to marinate for 3-4 hours at room temperature, so pre-prepare if you're making them for dinner with guests.

INGREDIENTS

- ½ lb (225g) of fresh baby Mozzarella balls (drained)
- 1 tbsp (15ml) of freshly chopped basil
- 1 tbsp (15ml) of fresh parsley
- 1 tbsp (15ml) freshly chopped oregano
- 3 tsp (45ml) of lemon juice
- ¼ tsp (1ml) salt
- ½ cup (125ml) of quality virgin olive oil

METHOD

1. Put the oregano, parsley, lemon juice, basil and salt in an airtight container or a zip-seal plastic bag. Gently swirl to combine.

2. Now add the drained baby mozzarella balls, re-seal lid or zip bag airtight and again swirl to cover the cheese balls.

3. Set aside the mozzarella balls in the marinade at room temperature for at least 4 hours. Then drain and serve on a white serving plate for maximum effect.

Succulent TOMATO, GORGONZOLA & GREEN OLIVE SKEWERS

Serves	6
Prep time	10m
Total time	10m

I often make this quick simple snack as a starter, a prelude to a tasty pasta, or as a mid-evening bite when thowing a buffet party. The skewered mix of flavours and textures are so juicy and tasty and are best eaten immediately after preparation or chilled before eating.

INGREDIENTS

- 12 firm and sweet baby bell tomatoes
- 12 large ripe green pitted olives
- ¼ pound (110g) block of good Italian blue cheese (Gorgonzola)

METHOD

1. Wash and dry the olives and tomatoes. Then set aside.

2. Chop the cheese into cubes about 1" (25mm) squares.

3. Now skewer though the middle starting with the olive, cheese and then tomato. I like to use palm skewers, but simple wooden ones will do the job just as well.

Tantalizing TARTS WITH HAM, BASIL MELON AND FIGS

Serves	6
Prep time	15m
Cook time	30m
Total time	45m

These scrumptious tartlets draw together ingredients that are each very distinctive in their own way. There is the contrast of the salty Parma ham and the sweet figs. The marshmallow like softness of the figs and melon, versus the crispiness of the filo shells. Yet combined, they form an incredibly light Italian snack!

INGREDIENTS

- 1 x 270g (10oz) pack of filo pastry, cut into 6 x 3" (75mm) squares and crimp each upwards into shell tartlets as the main image
- 2 ripe and fresh figs
- 1 small honeydew or cantaloupe melon made into 6 x 25mm (1") balls
- 3 slices of Parma ham (with fat removed)
- Handful of basil leaves

METHOD

Cut the thawed filo sheet into 6 x 3" (75mm) squares and crimp each upwards into shell tartlets as the main image. Cook in a pre-heated oven for 30 minutes at 200C/400F or until light golden brown

1. Wash and peel the figs, saving some to slice for decoration. Cut them in slices. Weight the other ingredients and divide everything in 3 portions.
2. Roll a slice of Parma ham into a cone and insert one in each filo shell. Next, add a melon ball, then add two figs slices, using your creative flair to make them look great, with a few leaves of basil to complete your masterpiece!

"

wherever I go, I am Italian. The way I talk. The way I eat. The way femininity is important to me. The way I love Italian food.

"

--- MONICA BELLUCCI

Marvellous FRIED MOZZARELLA WITH TOMATO & OREGANO SAUCE

Serves	4
Prep time	35m
Cook time	30m
Total time	1h 5m

This snack is visually great and tastes as good as it looks. The crisp golden mozzarella sticks are served alongside a mouth-watering sauce and make a fantastic light lunch or starter.

INGREDIENTS

FOR THE MOZZARELLA

- 4 thin slices of white bread, no crusts
- 3-4 finely chopped basil leaves
- 125ml (½ cup) of milk
- 250g (9oz) of mozzarella
- 2 beaten eggs
- Oil – for frying

FOR THE SAUCE

- 400g (1lb) tin of Italian whole tomatoes
- 2 tbsp (30ml) of virgin olive oil
- Optional ½ mild onion or ginger, chopped finely
- 125ml (½ cup) white wine
- ½ tsp (2.5ml) dried oregano
- Handful of coarsely chopped basil leaves

METHOD

1. To make the sauce: Heat the olive oil in a frying pan and fry the optional onion or ginger for a minute on a medium heat.

2. Add the tomatoes to the pan, then the wine and oregano and bring to the boil. Now reduce the heat and simmer for 20 minutes. Set aside and cool slightly.

3. Add the sauce to a blender or food processor, season with salt and pepper. Pulse for a few seconds, taking care not to completely liquidise the mix. Now add the basil leaves to the sauce mix.

4. Gently toast both sides of the bread slices, then crumble into fine breadcrumbs. Mix the breadcrumbs with the beaten eggs and set aside.

5. Cut the mozzarella into finger size sticks, season with salt and pepper and coat with the breadcrumb mix

6. Heat the oil in a deep-fat fryer and when hot, deep fry the coated mozzarella sticks for about 4 minutes until crisp and golden. Drain the sticks on kitchen paper

7. To serve: heat the sauce and serve as a side dipping dish. Place the fried mozzarella sticks on a serving dish and eat immediately.

Astounding ASPARAGUS WRAPPED IN BACON

Serves	6
Prep time	10m
Cook time	12m
Total time	22m

Best made when seasonal asparagus is available, with this easy starter recipe.

INGREDIENTS

- Two bunches of asparagus spears (about 20 in total) Remove fibrous ends
- 2 tbsp (30ml) of olive oil
- Fistful of fresh mint leaves chopped roughly
- 8 slices of thinly sliced smoked back bacon or pancetta
- Zest of 1 lemon
- 6 sweet baby tomatoes and a handful of parsley to garnish

METHOD

1. Preheat the oven to 200C (400F)
2. Cook the asparagus spears in boiling salted water for 2 minutes, drain, then set aside
3. Crush the mint with the oil and lemon zest and coat mix on to the asparagus
4. Put together in thee asparagus spears and wrap with the bacon rasher.
5. Place on a baking tray and roast for 12 minutes or until the bacon is crisp
6. Garnish with halved baby tomatoes, parsley leaves and a sprinkle of sea salt

Brilliant BRUSCHETTA, TOMATO & BASIL

Serves	8
Prep time	20m
Grill time	10m
Total time	30m

I often use this quick simple snack as a starter, a prelude to a tasty pasta, or as a mid-evening bite when thowing a buffet party. They are so crunchy and tasty and are best eaten after the baguette slices come out of the grill. The best and quickest way to toast the baguette slices is to use a sandwich toaster, because it cooks both sides at the same time. I first came across this tasty snack in the Italian city of Milan.

INGREDIENTS

- 2 fresh long bruschetta bread rolls
- 6 large fresh sweet tomatoes
- 1 handful of fresh basil leaves
- 1 tbsp of rock salt
- ¼ cup of virgin olive oil

METHOD

1. Wash, dry and take the leaves of the basil sprigs and coarsely chop. Then set aside.

2. In a small mixing bowl, add the olive oil, half of the basil and half of the salt. Then stir gently and set aside. Next, chop the tomatoes thinly and set aside ready for adding later.

3. Slice the bruschetta loaf at a slight angle and make each slice quite thin, about 6 to 8mm (¼"). Then lightly toast both sides until golden brown – not burnt. Once toasted, leave on a baking tray. On each mini toast, add a slice of tomato (should cover most of the toast), then sprinkle a twist of freshly ground rock salt over each tomato, add a light sprinkling of the remaining fresh basil on each completed toasty, then drizzle a tsp of the basil oil mix on the top and serve immediately.

Homemade SPINACH & CHEESE DUMPLINGS

Serves	10
Prep time	25m
Cook time	10m
Total time	35m

I have been making 'gnocchi Verdi' for many years. It is an immensely satisfying simple dish to make and a perfect starter for almost any Italian main course. The bonus is that it can also be used as a light main course too!

INGREDIENTS

- 80ml (⅓ cup) of macaroni pasta
- 60g (¼ cup) water
- 30ml (2 tbsp) semi skimmed milk
- 180ml (¾ cup) of mature grated cheddar cheese
- Pinch of salt and black pepper mix to taste

TOPPING

- ¼ cup of melted butter
- ½ cup of grated Parmesan cheese

METHOD

1. Fry the optional onion in butter until tender, or substitute with finely chopped ginger. Now add spinach; cook and stir over a medium heat until the juice has evaporated. add the ricotta and stir and cook for 4 minutes. Set aside in a large bowl.

2. Mix in ¾ cup of flour and Parmesan cheese. Leave to cool for 5 minutes and set aside.

3. Stir in the eggs and mix well. Add the remaining flour to a bowl. Drop the mix by tbspfuls into flour; roll lightly to coat and shape each into an oval.

4. In a large saucepan, bring water and chicken stock cube to boil; then reduce heat. Add a third of the dumplings at a time, simmer, for 8-10 minutes. Remove with a slotted spoon; cover to keep warm. Lightly cover with butter; dusting each ball with Parmesan. Serve immediately.

Gorgeous PARMA HAM & FRESH FRUITS

Serves	8
Prep time	15m
Total time	15m

This mouth-wateringly tasty treat has been a summer favourite of mine. It is really quick and easy to make and such a delight to eat. I hope you enjoy this tasty starter or snack as much as I do. For more guests, just adjust the recipe accordingly.

INGREDIENTS

- 2 cored pears cut into 16 wedges
- Half a cantaloupe melon cut into thin wedges
- 16 Mini - baby sweet tomatoes
- 16 thin slices of prosciutto ham
- 4 kiwi fruits, peeled and sliced
- ¼ cup honey
- 2 tbsp (30ml) of coarse sea salt

METHOD

1. Place a slice of the ham on flat surface and roll it up in to a tube, then place the rest of the rolled-up ham tubes equally radiating around the outside of a serving plate.

2. Place a pear wedge and melon wedge between each prosciutto roll and alongside that towards the outside of the plate insert a Kiwi wedge. Drizzle honey over the top of the wedges.

3. Add the baby tomatoes around the plate using your artistic discretion. Sprinkle all around with some coarse sea salt.

4. Eat immediately or chill for up to 24 hours

Tasty # FRESH HOMEMADE TOMATO & BASIL SOUP

Serves	6
Prep time	15m
Cook time	30m
Total time	45m

This recipe is so much tastier than any tinned or packet soup and the best part is...it doesn't have a hint of garlic in it! If you can't eat onion, then simply replace it with the fresh grated ginger in the recipe. It's great to eat any season of the year.

INGREDIENTS

- 725g (1½ lbs) fresh tomatoes, chopped
- 1 mild onion (optional) chopped.
- 2 tbsp (30ml) of freshly grated ginger
- 475ml (1 pint) chicken stock
- 1 handful of basil leaves chopped roughly.
- 2 tbsp (30ml) butter
- 2 tbsp (30ml) plain flour
- 1 tsp (15ml) salt
- 2 tsp (30ml) brown sugar to taste

METHOD

1. In a frying pan, sauté the onions or ginger on a medium heat for about 10 minutes, taking care not to burn them.

2. Then, in a large saucepan, over medium heat, add the tomatoes, onion (or ginger) and chicken stock. Bring to the boil and cook gently for about 20 minutes to blend all of the flavours. Remove from the hob and push the mixture though a sieve into a large saucepan. Remove anything left in the sieve.

3. In the now empty saucepan, melt the butter over medium heat, gently stirring in the flour to make a thick paste, cooking until the mixture is a medium brown. Gently whisk in some of the sieved tomato mixture, so that no lumps form, then stir in the balance. Season with a little sugar and salt to taste. Serve immediately.

"
There is nothing more romantic than Italian food.

"

--- ELISHA CUTHBERT

IL SECONDO

(SECOND MEAL OR MAIN)

PORK

Tasty

RIGATONI PASTA WITH A TOMATO & PANCETTA SAUCE

Serves	4
Prep time	15m
Cook time	45m
Total time	1h

I first experienced this mouth-watering dish in a restaurant in Rome. It is such a tasty meal and nutritious too, yet so quick and easy to make. I hope you enjoy it.

INGREDIENTS

- 450g (1lb) rigatoni pasta
- 5 tbsp olive oil plus extra for drizzling
- 1 onion (optional) finely chopped, or replace with finely chopped ginger
- 200g (7oz)pancetta diced

- 2 x 350g (14oz) cans plum tomatoes
- 2 tbsp tomato paste
- 1 pinch sugar
- 1 tbsp flat leaf parsley chopped

- 1 sprig rosemary
- 56g (2oz) parmesan cheese grated
- Coarse salt & freshly ground black pepper

METHOD

1. To prepare basic tomato sauce, heat olive oil (4 tbsp) in a pan over a medium heat.

2. Add the optional onion (or substitute a small chopped fresh ginger) and cook for 5 minutes.

3. Add chopped tomatoes to the pan along with the tomato paste, sugar and rosemary. Lower the heat and simmer for 30 – 35 minutes.

4. Bring a large pan of water to the boil and add salt and the rigatoni. Reduce the heat, then simmer according to the packet instructions, until al dente.

5. Heat the remaining oil in a large frying pan over a medium heat. Add the pancetta and cook, turning occasionally until it is golden brown on all sides.

6. Add the tomato sauce to the pancetta, reduce the heat to low and simmer for 3 – 4 minutes.

7. Now drain the rigatoni pasta and add it to the tomato sauce. season to taste.

8. Stir in the parsley and serve immediately with Parmesan and a splattering of olive oil.

Delicate

SLOW COOKED PORK CHOPS WITH PASTA & TOMATO SAUCE

Serves	4
Prep time	25m
Oven time	2h 30m
Total time	2h 55m

This mouth-wateringly tasty traditional lightly seasoned slow cooked pork chop meal is cooked in a rich, thick tomato sauce for a delicious dinner any time of the year. Great to impress friends and family!

INGREDIENTS

- 2 tsp extra-virgin olive oil
- 4 bone-in pork chops 25-30mm (1" to 1½) thick
- 1 tsp salt divided
- ½ tsp black pepper divided
- 1 350g (14.5oz) can chopped tomatoes with juice
- 150g (6oz) of tomato paste
- 1 small green bell pepper seeded and chopped
- (Optional) ½ small onion chopped (½ - ¾ cup) or add ginger below
- 1 25mm (1") clump of fresh ginger finely grated
- 1 tbsp dried oregano
- ¼ tsp red pepper flakes (optional)
- Cooked spaghetti or fettuccine noodles, grated Parmesan cheese, chopped fresh parsley

METHOD

1. Heat olive oil in a large frying pan sauté and over medium-high heat.

2. Season pork chops with ½ tsp salt and ¼ tsp black pepper. Sear the pork chops in shallow frying pan for 3 minutes each side, to form a light crust. Now put the pork chops into a casserole dish. Pre-heat the oven at 140C (275F).

3. Add the remaining ingredients to the casserole dish, stir gently to combine.

4. Cover and cook on low for 2 – 2½ hours, until pork chops are tender and cooked though.

5. Serve over spaghetti or fettuccine noodles with sauce spooned on top, sprinkled with Parmesan cheese and garnish with fresh parsley.

Splendid SPAGHETTI CARBONARA WITH HAM

Serves	4
Prep time	20m
Cook time	30m
Total time	50m

Carbonara is a Roman pasta dish whose recipe has been passed down though generations of Italian families. It is so creamy and cheesy and such a quick wholesome meal to make for families and friends.

INGREDIENTS

- 450g (1lb) of fresh spaghetti
- 2 tbsp of extra virgin olive oil
- 120g (4oz) of pancetta or back bacon, cut into small strips
- 60g (4oz) of fresh finely chopped ginger
- 2 large eggs
- Freshly ground pepper
- Handful of fresh parsley
- 250ml (1 cup) of freshly grated parmesan cheese

METHOD

1. Boil a large pot of salted water (add salt once boiling), add the pasta and cook for 8 to 10 minutes al dente. Drain the pasta, keeping ½ a cup of the pasta's cooking water to use in the sauce later as needed.

2. Now, heat the olive oil in a deep frying pan on medium heat. Next, add the pancetta or bacon, and sauté for about 4 m', until the strips are crisp. Now add the ginger into the fat and sauté for no longer than a minute.

3. Meanwhile, add the drained spaghetti to the pan and fold in for 2 minutes to coat the strands in the pancetta fat.

4. Now, beat the eggs and parmesan together in a mixing bowl, avoiding lumps by stirring well. Take the pan from the hob and pour the cheese and egg mixture into the pasta, whisking quickly until the eggs thicken, but do not scramble (this is why it's done off the hob to make sure it doesn't happen).

5. Finally, thin the sauce with a drop of the remaining pasta water, until it meets your preferred thickness. Season the carbonara with freshly ground black pepper and coarse salt to taste. Pile the spaghetti carbonara into pre-warmed serving bowls and garnish with chopped parsley. Enjoy!

Perfect PORK CHOP AGRODOLCE

Serves	4
Prep time	20m
Rice prep	30m
Total time	50m

Pork chops for me evoke childhood memories of that gorgeous decadent aroma wafting though the house while cooking. How can you resist those crispy fat edges? The crumbly meat falling off the bone? Inexpensive, pork chops were a staple diet in my household and my mother would buy them regularly. So simple to cook, just season and straight in the pan to brown. What could be simpler?

But this Italian take on good old home cooking I guarantee will be a friend pleaser at any dinner occasion. Pork Chop Agrodolce is simply pork chops, bathed in a sweet and sour sauce. This Italian take on the venerable pork chop is one of my favourites and I hope you will feel the same too.

INGREDIENTS

- 125ml (½ cup) balsamic vinegar
- 60g (2½ oz) of fresh ginger chopped finely
- 4 sprigs thyme
- 4 tbsp honey
- 3 tbsp butter, at room temperature
- 4 boned pork loin chops, about 300g (12oz) each
- 1 tsp coarse salt
- Pinch of freshly ground black pepper
- 2 tbsp of virgin olive oil

METHOD

1. In a small saucepan, mix the balsamic vinegar, ginger and thyme sprigs. Place over medium heat and bring to a simmer. Continue to simmer until reduced by half, about 5 minutes. Add the honey and simmer another 3 to 4 minutes or until the mixture has thickened slightly. Stir in the butter and set aside

2. Preheat a frying pan over medium high heat.

3. Season the pork chops evenly on both sides with the salt and pepper. Add a splattering of olive oil and place on the hot frying pan. Grill for 5 minutes on the first side or until nicely browned. Flip the chops and grill for an additional 5 minutes on the second side. Baste the chops with some of the sauce and continue to baste and flip for an additional 5 minutes or until the outside of the meat is caramelized and slightly charred. Remove the chops to a platter and allow to rest for 10 minutes. Serve drizzled with the remaining sauce

I am a sucker for those old traditional places and Rome is as good as it gets, particularly when you thow in Italian food

--- ROGER FEDERER

Incredible ITALIAN SAUSAGE & EGG BAKE

Serves	6
Prep time	15m
Cook time	45m
Total time	1h

An Italian family staple, this is my ultimate version of this great Italian sausage and egg bake that I have perfected over the years. Simple to cook and mouth-wateringly tasty this main course has always been a firm favourite amongst friends. It is so quick and easy to make and so rewarding to eat. Simply season to taste and eat straight from the oven.

INGREDIENTS

- 454g (1lb) good garlic free pork sausages, skins removed and cut randomly into 25 to 50mm (1" to 2") slices
- ½ small rustic style white bread loaf, cut in to random 10mm to 25mm (½ to 1") cubes
- 2 tbsp extra-virgin olive oil

- 1 optional medium onion, finely diced or substitute for 60g (2½ oz) of fresh grated ginger
- 1 150g (6oz) tin or pack of sun dried tomatoes (non-garlic) in olive oil, drained and chopped into randomly sized pieces

- One pack of fresh baby spinach washed and drained
- 2 tbsp fresh basil ripped and chopped
- 2ml (½ tsp) salt
- 1ml (¼ tsp) freshly ground black pepper, plus extra for seasoning

- 6 large free-range eggs
- 130g (5oz) of goat's cheese, randomly crumbled

METHOD

1. Pre-heat your oven to 200C (400F)

2. Mix the bread cubes in with 1 tbsp of olive oil then spread evenly on stick proof baking sheet, on a shallow baking tray. Bake in the pre-heated oven for about 8 -10 minutes or until they just turn a gorgeous light brown colour. Remove from oven and reserve for later.

3. Now in a separate frying pan on a medium heat, add the remaining olive oil add the optional onion or ginger. After 1 minute, add the sausage slices and cook though for between 6 to 8 minutes. Now add the baby spinach, stirring often. Now add the basil and sun-dried tomatoes.

4. Now season with a pinch of both freshly ground coarse salt and black pepper.

5. Evenly spread the pan-fried mix into a medium sized baking dish. Place the baked bread cubes evenly across the top of the mix, then scatter the crumbled goat's cheese across the mix. You can now seal the top with plastic film and chill for up to two days before cooking or put straight into the oven to cook.

6. Just before you put the mixture into the oven, crack an egg into equal sixth segments on top of the mix, taking care not to break the yolks. Season with freshly ground salt and black pepper. Bake only once the egg whites are set, but the yolks are still looking runny (normally 10-15 minutes) or if you prefer your yolks set hard about 20 minutes. Eat immediately straight from the oven to table.

Fantastic PENNE PASTA WITH HAM & BASIL

Serves	6
Prep time	20m
Cook time	20m
Total time	40m

This is a very easy and delicious authentic Italian recipe. Fresh pasta is much nicer than dried, but either will do. Just follow the pack instructions for cooking. You can make double the amount and refrigerate half for later in the week. Great for those of us leading busy lives, but want the healthiest, tastiest meals in a flash.

INGREDIENTS

- 1 pack 450g (1lb) of fresh penne pasta
- 750g (3 cups) of cooked ham, cut into 12mm (½") cubes
- 3 tbsp of butter
- 1½ tsp of fresh finely chopped basil, reserving a handful of whole leaves to garnish.

- 60ml (¼ cup) of finely chopped fresh parsley
- 60ml (¼ cup) of extra virgin olive oil
- 125ml (½ cup) of grated Parmesan cheese
- ½ tsp of dried oregano
- 400ml (14oz) of good quality chicken stock

- 1 tbsp lemon juice
- 60g (2oz) of coarsely chopped large brown mushrooms
- 30g (1oz) of freshly grated ginger
- 1 large sweet bell red pepper chopped finely

METHOD

1. Cook the pasta according to the pack instructions for 'al dente' firmness. Then drain.

2. Now, using a large frying pan, heat both the oil and butter over a medium heat. Add the red pepper, ginger, mushrooms and stir for about 5 minutes until the ham is brown and the pepper, ginger and mushrooms are tender.

3. Now add the herbs and cook for a further 2 minutes, stirring constantly.

4. Add the lemon juice and chicken stock and bring to a boil, then reduce heat to simmer, without a lid, for a further 15 minutes, reducing the liquid by 50%.

5. Add the pasta and gently combine all ingredients, serve in pre-warmed pasta bowls, Garnish with a few whole basil leaves and sprinkle with Parmesan cheese. Enjoy.

Succulent CARBONARA FETTUCCINE

Serves	4
Prep time	10m
Cook time	15m
Total time	25m

If you are looking for a delicious quick meal that is ready in less than half an hour from scratch, then this Italian classic is the meal for you. When you can prepare and make such a tasty garlic free meal in 25 minutes, why do so many people bother with processed food?

INGREDIENTS

- 350g (¾ lb) fresh fettuccine pasta
- 30g (1 oz) butter
- 225g (½ lb) back bacon rashers, chopped randomly
- 50mm (2") clump of freshly ginger, grated
- 30ml (2 tbsp) fresh rosemary finely chopped
- 125ml (½ cup) light thickened cooking cream
- 80ml (⅓ cup) parmesan, finely grated
- Salt and freshly ground black pepper to season
- 2 eggs
- 2 egg yolks

METHOD

1. Cook the fresh pasta according to the packet directions

2. Now, on a medium heat, melt the butter in a large saucepan and add the chopped bacon. Cook to a light golden colour (about 5 minutes).

3. Add the ginger and rosemary, stirring constantly for about 1 minute.

4. Now drain the pasta and return to saucepan. Add both the egg and bacon mixtures to the pasta. Heat for a minute, folding gently over low heat until sauce thickens and sticks to the pasta. Serve hot immediately.

"

Ideas are like pizza dough, made to be tossed around.

"

--- ANNA QUINDLEN

BEEF

Classic **LASAGNE**

Serves	6-8
Prep time	40m
Cook time	50m
Total time	1h 30m

Making a lasagne takes time, passion dedication. But the rewards are obvious in every tasty mouthful. This original lasagne recipe is robust, comforting and will leave you craving more. Isn't that what all good food should be about?

INGREDIENTS

- 2 tbsp olive oil for frying
- 250g (5oz) pack fresh lasagne sheets
- 50g (2oz) prosciutto, randomly chopped

FOR THE MEAT SAUCE

- 700g (1½ lb) free-range beef mince
- 1 large celery stick finely chopped
- 1 onion, finely chopped (optional)
- Small fresh ginger finely chopped
- 2 tbsp tomato purée
- 230g (9oz) tin chopped Italian tomatoes
- 150ml (⅔ cup) quality beef stock
- 1 tbsp fresh finely chopped oregano
- Small bunch fresh basil, leaves picked and ripped into small pieces

FOR THE BÉCHAMEL SAUCE

- 700ml (1¼ pints) whole milk
- 60g (2oz) unsalted butter
- 60g (2oz) plain flour
- 80g (¾ cup) parmesan, finely grated
- Pinch freshly grated nutmeg

METHOD

1. Heat the oil in a large frying pan over a medium-high heat, then add the prosciutto and fry until crisp. Reserve to a plate using a slotted spoon.

2. Meat Sauce. Add the celery and onion (or ginger) to the pan with a pinch of salt and pepper; cook until soft (about 5-10 minutes).

3. Add the mince and fry for a further 5 minutes until lightly browned, breaking up any clumps.

4. Add in the tomato purée, stir in the chopped tomatoes; cook for a further minute.

5. Add the stock and then simmer for 40 minutes over a low heat until the sauce has thickened.

6. Remove from the heat, season with salt and pepper, then stir in the fried prosciutto, chopped oregano and most of the basil leaves.

7. Béchamel sauce. Heat the butter in a medium saucepan over a medium to high heat. Add flour, stirring constantly for about 4 minutes until the mixture starts to thicken and change colour. Gently pour in the milk, whisking continuously for about 7 minutes until the milky sauce has thickened.

8. Take off the heat. Now stir in 20g (¾ oz) of the parmesan and the nutmeg, seasoning well with salt and pepper. Heat the oven to 200C (400F).

9. To construct your masterpiece, spread a thin layer of the béchamel sauce over the base of the baking dish, then cover with lasagne sheets just overlapping. Then pour over a third of the residual béchamel sauce, sprinkle a little of the grated cheese over mixture and top with half the meat sauce. Now cover with another layer of lasagne sheets, top with half the remaining white sauce, then all the remaining meat sauce. Add the last layer of lasagne sheets, then cover with the rest of the béchamel sauce. sprinkle the remaining grated cheese over the whole of the top layer of sauce.

10. Bake the lasagne for 40-45 minutes until golden brown and simmering. Garnish with the remaining basil and serve immediately.

Juicy

ITALIAN MEATBALLS IN A RICH TOMATO SAUCE

Serves	4
Prep time	20m
Cook time	2h
Total time	2h 20m

This is a very easy and delicious recipe. Homemade meatballs are much nicer than shop bought and the same goes for the tomato sauce too. You can make double the amount and refrigerate half for later in the week. In fact, the second half always seem to taste so much better after leaving the meatballs to marinate in the rich sauce over a few days in the fridge.

INGREDIENTS

FOR THE MEATBALLS

- 500g (1lb) of lean minced/ground beef
- 25mm (1") of fresh ginger - grated
- 1 cup fresh breadcrumbs
- 1 tsp of grated parmesan cheese
- 1 tsp of dried parsley
- 1 tsp of ground black pepper
- 2.5ml (½ tsp) of oregano
- 1 tbsp of olive oil
- 1 egg, beaten

FOR THE SAUCE

- 500g (1 pint) of tomato passata
- 1 crumbly chicken stock cube
- 125ml (½ cup) of drinkable red wine
- 1 chopped and fried mild shallot (optional)
- 2.5ml (½ tsp) of dried basil
- Salt and ground pepper to taste
- 2.5ml (½ tsp) of brown or demerara sugar
- 2.5ml (½ tsp) of oregano

METHOD

1. In a large mixing bowl, blend the beef, breadcrumbs, parmesan cheese, parsley, oregano, and black pepper. Mix with your hands until all ingredients are combined. Roll out into small balls about 30mm (1¼") in diameter. Now set aside on a greaseproof paper lined baking tray.

2. In a large saucepan, add the olive oil and fry the shallot (if using) until soft and transparent, not burnt. Now stir in the wine and simmer for 1 minute to ensure that most of the alcohol evaporates.

3. While on a medium heat, add the tomatoes, crumble the stock cube in the mix, add the oregano, the sugar and the basil. Simmer for half an hour.

4. Now add a tbsp of olive oil in the frying pan and on a high heat, fry the meatballs in batches until each meatball is lightly browned all over. You may need to do this in 2 or 3 batches.

5. Next, add the meatballs to the sauce, bring to the boil, then immediately lower the heat to simmer for a further 1½ hours. Place the lid on the saucepan, stirring gently every 10-15 minutes.

6. Now serve, either with pasta, spaghetti or on its own, with a sprinkling of grated parmesan and ground black pepper to taste.

Hearty **BEEF CANNELLONI**

Serves	6
Prep time	45m
Hob time	20m
Total time	1h 5m

This is a quick and easy to make, simple, but tantalisingly tasty beef cannelloni. It's a classic Italian dish that has stood the test of time and never fails to amaze. The wine adds a hearty richness to the minced beef filling like no other. I hope you enjoy this great meal.

INGREDIENTS

- 450g (1lb) lean mince
- 250ml (1 cup) olive oil
- 2 400g (1lb) tins whole plum tomatoes
- 1 onion thinly sliced (optional) or substitute for small ginger finely grated
- ¼ tsp (1ml) dried sage
- ¼ tsp (1ml) dried rosemary
- 125ml (½ cup) white wine
- 12 cannelloni
- Salt and pepper to taste
- Béchamel sauce (Page 44)

METHOD

1. Beef sauce filling: using a large frying pan on a medium heat, heat the oil and sauté the beef with the onion, sage and rosemary; break up any clumps of mince with a wooden spoon. Cook until the meat is evenly browned and crumbly. Add a pinch of salt and pepper, then add the white wine; cook until the wine is evaporated.

2. To make the béchamel sauce: Follow the instructions in the previous Lasagne recipe on page 42 and set aside.

3. Melt 30g (1oz) butter in a medium saucepan over medium heat and sauté the optional onion or ginger until soft and tender. Add the remaining 125ml (½ cup) of white wine and cook until it evaporates; add tomatoes and salt. Mix well; then simmer for 15 minutes.

4. Boil a large pan of lightly salted water. Now add the cannelloni tubes, a few at a time, and cook until al dente; then using a slotted spoon, remove immediately into a pan filled with cold water. Lift pasta out with slotted spoon and arrange on a flat surface or board.

5. Pre-heat oven to 200C (400F) / Gas 5.

6. Insert the meat filling into each tube, starting from one end and using your finger to push the meat paste into each shell. Lay each filled tube in a large baking dish and then pour on the béchamel sauce and sprinkle with grated mozzarella cheese.

7. Bake in preheated oven for 25 minutes or until heated though. Allow to stand for 5 minutes, then serve.

Authentic TAGLIATELLE ALLA BOLOGNESE

Serves	4
Prep time	30m
Hob time	3h
Total time	3h 30m

ORIGINAL RECIPE FROM BOLOGNA!

After carrying out a long drawn out investigation and research, on October 17, 1982, the Bolognese chapter of the Accademia Italiana della Cucina, announced this recipe as the official method to create true Bolognese sauce. Although I am certain that each Italian family will have their own recipe. I found this authentic method a few years ago and have since found that no variation betters it. Best of all, like so many truly authentic Italian recipes, there is no garlic to be seen! You can add a small amount of optional onion for added authentic flavour. If onion is out of bounds, substitute it for the ginger option.

In Italy, Bolognese sauce is rarely served with spaghetti since it tends to slip off the pasta and remain on the plate. In its place, the people of Bologna traditionally serve their celebrated meat sauce with tagliatelle.

Genuine Bolognese contains no tomato sauce, but I have added a handful of sun dried tomatoes that adds an additional layer of flavour and trace of sweetness to what is a complex fusion of flavours. Bolognese is epitomised by its long, slow cooking. In this case, it starts with simmering the meat in milk (to lower any sharpness of the sun-dried tomatoes added later) and red wine.

INGREDIENTS

FOR THE SAUCE

- 200g (10½ oz) of good quality ground/minced beef

- 100g (5oz) of good quality ground/minced pork

- 150g (5oz) pancetta - unsmoked

- 50g (2oz) onion – minced (or use ginger below)

- 50g (2oz) ginger – minced (instead of onion above)

- 50g (2oz) celery – minced or finely diced

- 50g (2oz) carrot – minced or finely diced

- ½ glass of drinkable red wine (if it tastes bad, don't use it!)

- 30g (1oz) concentrated tomato puree/paste

- 180ml (¾ cup) of fresh semi-skimmed or whole milk

- 28G (1oz) Porcini mushrooms (dried)

- Handful of sun dried tomatoes

- Olive oil

- Sea salt and pepper

ADDITION

- 150g (5oz) fresh tagliatelle

- Sea salt to flavour

METHOD

1. Fry the pancetta lightly in a few tsp of olive oil until its fat starts to seep out. Do not over-fry.

2. Add the vegetables and fry, stirring occasionally until the onions are transparent.

3. Now add the beef and pork mince until it is lightly browned, ensuring there are no clumps of meat.

4. Add the tomato puree/paste.

5. Now add the milk, drop by drop, until it is absorbed completely

6. Season with ground black pepper and sea salt.

7. Cover and cook for 3 hours so that the sauce simmers, stirring very occasionally. Add milk if it starts to look dry.

8. Serve with freshly cooked tagliatelle (don't succumb to serving with spaghetti)

9. You can toss the pasta with a knob of butter and then add a touch of grated parmesan cheese before adding to the delicious sauce.

Crispy RAGU PASTA BAKE

Serves	4
Prep time	45m
Cook time	30m
Total time	1h 15m

This mouth-wateringly tasty pasta bake is always a firm favourite with friends and family. It is so quick and easy to make and so scrumptious to eat. I hope you enjoy this delectable meal as much as I do.

INGREDIENTS

- 450g (1lb) of lean mince/ground beef
- 2 tbsp of olive oil
- 1 pinch of freshly ground black pepper
- 1 finely chopped carrot
- 1 finely chopped celery stick
- 3 bay leaves

- 125ml (½ cup) of dry roasted breadcrumbs
- 25mm (1") ginger or 1 optional finely chopped mild shallot
- 250ml (1 cup) of red wine
- 2 400g (12oz) tins of chopped Italian tomatoes

- 250g (9oz) of pasta shells or tubes
- 250g (9oz) grated mozzarella
- 1 tsp of dried oregano
- A sprig of basil leaves chopped roughly

METHOD

1. Heat a large frying pan and add oil. Brown the meat on a high heat for 8-10 minutes. Now transfer on a side plate and set aside. Add another tbsp of olive oil on a medium heat and fry the onions, celery and carrot until soft and transparent but not browned. Season with salt and pepper to flavour.

2. Now add the bay leaves and stir gently in with the cooked meat. Now add the red wine and let it simmer and gently bubble for a few minutes, then pour in the tomatoes and simmer for about 20-25 minutes with the lid on the pan, stirring every 5 minutes.

3. Now heat the oven to 200C (400F) and then fill a saucepan large enough to take all the pasta, with hot water. Add a tsp of ground sea salt and bring to the boil. Now cook the pasta for a further 3 minutes only.

4. Drain pasta and arrange the tubes or shells in a large 2L (½ gallon) baking dish and then ladle on the sauce, ensuring that all the tubes or shells are filled. Next, sprinkle the grated mozzarella over the top and be quite generous with the amount that you use.

5. Now mix the breadcrumbs and oregano with a tbsp of olive oil and then evenly scatter the mix over the pasta and cheese topping. Finish off with a liberal coating of parmesan cheese. Bake for 25 minutes or when it's a lovely golden crispy finish. Sprinkle basil leaves on top and serve immediately

Juicy

BEEF FILLET WITH WILD MUSHROOM

Serves	6
Prep time	30m
Oven time	1h 20m
Total time	1h 50m

This fantastic main course is without doubt amongst family and friend's favourites. It does take a little time to prepare, but believe me, it is worth the wait. Cooking the fillet beef in a cocoon of Parma ham and mushroom filling, makes for the most tasty, moist and flavoursome steak that you could imagine. Paired with my vegetable recommendation, you cannot fail to impress your guests.

INGREDIENTS

- 1 kg (2.2lb) trimmed fillet of beef
- 1 grated 50mm (2") chunk of fresh ginger
- 50g (2oz) unsalted butter
- 28g (1oz) dried wild mushrooms or porcini
- 10 large slices Parma ham or prosciutto
- 5 sprigs of fresh thyme
- ½ a lemon
- Rapeseed oil or olive oil
- 4 sprigs of fresh rosemary
- 250ml (1 cup) drinkable red wine (if it tastes bad cold, it will taste bad hot!)

METHOD

1. Preheat the oven to 220C (425F) and position rack centrally.

2. Allow meat to get to room temperature for at least 30 minutes prior to cooking.

3. Fill a mixing jug with 500ml (1 pint) of boiling water and add the dried wild mushrooms. After about 20 minutes, drain and set aside.

4. Place a large frying pan over a high heat with 1 knob of butter. Add the wild mushrooms, grated ginger and 2 tbsp of water, then reduce the heat to low and simmer for 5 minutes, or until thick and syrupy.

5. Squeeze in the lemon juice and stir in the remaining butter, then season to taste with the pepper and sea salt. Leave to cool for a few minutes.

6. Drizzle 1 tbsp of oil over the beef and season with black pepper. Seal in a roasting tray over a medium heat on the hob until browned all over, then take of the heat.

7. Place the slices of Parma ham out on a large piece of non-stick baking paper so that they're just overlapping and big enough to wrap around the beef. Spread the hydrated mushrooms lengthways over the centre half of the prosciutto, then place the fillet of beef on top.

8. Now carefully roll up the meat and filling. Detach the paper and gather the ends of the Parma ham. Secure and tie with butcher's string.

9. Place in the oven and cook for 25 minutes for rare, 35 minutes for medium, or 45 minutes for well done. Once the meat has been cooking long enough for your choice of tenderness, place the meat on a chopping board to rest for 5 minutes, pouring any remaining juices back into the tray.

10. Now, heat the tray over a medium to high setting on the hob, add the wine and simmer to your desired thickness.

11. Remove from the hob, then pour the juices though a sieve before serving. Let the meat rest for at least 20 minutes before serving.

12. Carve the fillet roll and serve. Lightly pour over the red wine sauce. Optionally serve with roast potatoes and steamed greens on the side.

VEAL

Juicy OSSO BUCO BRAISED VEAL

Serves	6
Prep time	25m
Cook time	2h
Total time	2h 25m

This is an easy and delicious recipe. Homemade braised veal is so much nicer than shop bought. You can make double the amount and refrigerate half for later in the week. In fact, the second half always seem to taste so much better after leaving the meat to marinate in the rich sauce over a few days in the fridge.

INGREDIENTS

- 3 whole veal shanks (about 500g (1lb 2oz) per shank), trimmed
- 1 dry bay leaf
- 1 sprig fresh rosemary
- 1 sprig fresh thyme
- 1 small piece of fresh ginger finely chopped
- A good handful of pitted green olives
- Cheesecloth

- Kitchen twine, for bouquet garni and tying the veal shanks
- Sea salt and freshly ground black pepper
- Plain flour, for dipping the shanks in
- 125ml (½ cup) vegetable oil
- 1 small carrot diced into 1cm (½") cubes

- 1 stalk celery diced into 1cm (½") cubes
- 1 tbsp tomato paste
- 250ml (1 cup) dry white wine
- 750ml (3 cups) chicken stock
- 3 tbsp Chopped fresh flat-leaf Italian parsley
- 1 tbsp lemon zest

METHOD

1. Place the bay leaf, thyme and rosemary into the cheese cloth and secure with twine. This is your bouquet garni. Alternatively, you can buy this ready prepared with dried herbs, but fresh is best.

2. Pat dry the veal shanks with paper towels to remove any surplus moisture. This ensures that the Veal shanks brown easier. Secure the meat to the bone with the butchers or kitchen string. Use salt and freshly ground pepper to season. Then dip the shanks in the flour, shaking off any surplus.

3. Then, using a large casserole dish, heat the vegetable oil until smoke starts to rise. Add the tied shanks to the hot casserole dish and brown all sides, about 4 minutes per side. Now remove and set aside the browned shanks.

4. In the same dish, add the carrot, olives, ginger, and celery. Season with salt. This helps draw out the juices from the vegetables. Sauté until soft and clear, for 8 m.

5. Next, add the tomato paste and stir well. Return the browned shanks to the dish and slowly pour and mix in the white wine, reducing the liquid by half (5 m).

6. Add the bouquet garni and half of the chicken stock and bring to a boil. Now reduce the heat to low, cover dish and simmer for about 1½ hours or until the meat is falling off the bone. Check every 20 minutes or so, turning shanks and topping up the chicken stock as necessary. The cooking juices should always cover about ¾ of the shank.

7. Next, carefully remove the shanks from the pot and place on a serving dish. Remove the string from the shanks. Then dispose of the bouquet garni from the casserole dish.

8. Finally, pour all the sauce and juices from the casserole dish over the shanks. Top off the shanks with lemon zest and chopped parsley and serve immediately.

Brilliant COTOLETTA ALLA MILANESE

Serves	4
Prep time	15m
Cook time	10m
Total time	25m

This is a classic dish from the magnificent city of Milan that I first came across when working there. Similar in style to the ubiquitous German and Austrian wiener schnitzel, it differs in a few ways. Both are thinly pounded veal cutlets, breaded and pan-fried, although the Viennese version is traditionally dipped in both flour and breadcrumbs before frying, while the recipe from Milan is purely bread crumbs, cooked in butter.

INGREDIENTS

- 4 veal scallop's cutlets with bone
- Fine sea salt, to taste
- 2 large eggs, beaten
- 190ml (¾ cup) salted butter

- 125ml (½ cup) finely ground breadcrumbs lightly toasted in the oven
- Lemon wedges, for serving (optional)

- Sprigs of fresh parsley to dress (optional)

METHOD

1. Place the veal cutlets or scallops between two sheets of plastic film and beat with a wooden mallet to about 6mm (¼") thickness. If using bone-in cutlet: Trim the fat and make small cuts around the edges of the meat with the tip of a sharp knife to stop the chops from bending up as they fry.

2. Place the breadcrumbs and beaten eggs separately in 2 large bowls or rimmed plates.

3. Dry the meat by patting down with a paper towel, lightly salt, and then dip each scallop or chop first in the beaten egg, removing any surplus, then dip in the breadcrumbs, covering both sides and pressing down to make sure the crumbs stick. Remove any excess crumbs.

4. Now melt the butter in a large frying pan and when the foaming lessens, add the cutlets and cook quickly over a medium to high heat, turning to brown both sides.

5. Serve hot, dressed with parsley and lemon wedges

CHICKEN

Rustic ROMANA CHICKEN

Serves	4
Prep time	20m
Cook time	2h
Total time	2h 20m

Quick and easy to prepare and cook, this classic version of Rome's finest is a huge hit with everybody that has the pleasure to eat it. Using core Italian herbs and the ubiquitous chicken breast. How can it fail to tingle your taste buds?

INGREDIENTS

- 110g (4oz) of finely chopped washed and drained brown mushrooms
- 30g (1oz) of freshly grated ginger
- 125ml (½ cup) of dry white wine

- 4 170g (6oz) boneless chicken breasts cut into halves
- 2 tbsp of freshly chopped basil
- 1 tbsp fresh chopped thyme
- Pinch of ground pepper

- 1 tsp of salt
- 700g (2¼ cups) of chopped tinned Italian tomatoes
- 2 tbsp Olive oil
- Optional – two stalks of spring onion, finely chopped

METHOD

1. Heat olive oil in a large frying-pan over medium heat.
2. Add ginger and mushrooms, stirring occasionally cook for 3 minutes until tender,
3. Stir in chopped tomatoes, vinegar, wine, ½ tsp salt and a pinch of black pepper.
4. Bring to the boil. Reduce heat and simmer for 12 min until the sauce thickens, stirring occasionally.
5. Remove from heat.
6. Next add 1 tbsp basil.
7. Now pre-heat grill
8. In a small mixing bowl, mix the thyme, and the remaining tbsp basil, ⅛ tsp pepper and ½ tsp salt
9. Next, coat the chicken with remaining olive oil cooking then sprinkle with the thyme and basil mixture.
10. Grill for 5 minutes on each side or until it turns a nice golden brown.
11. Remove from grill, plate up and gently cover with tomato mixture and its ready to serve

Italian food is my favourite...
It's the most sophisticated
eating system.

--- PETER GABRIEL

Aromatic CHICKEN PARMESAN

Serves	6
Prep time	20m
Cook time	30m
Total time	50m

This is one of the finest crispy chicken breasts that you will see. Topped with homemade marinara sauce, parmesan cheese and melted mozzarella. Best served with very thin spaghetti.

INGREDIENTS

CHICKEN

- 2 large eggs
- 2 tbsp fresh chopped parsley
- 5ml (1 tsp) of dried oregano
- 3 good sized chicken breasts sliced horizontally to make 6 fillets
- 125ml (½ cup) fresh grated parmesan cheese
- 375ml (1½ cup) breadcrumbs (golden or Italian)
- 5 ml (1 tsp) of dried ginger
- Salt and pepper to season
- 125ml (½ cup) of olive oil

SAUCE

- 1 tbsp olive oil
- 1 optional medium onion chopped or replace with a 50mm (2") chunk of grated ginger
- 400g (14oz) tomato Passata
- Salt and pepper to season
- 5ml (1 tsp) dried oregano
- 5ml (1 tsp) dried basil
- 5ml (1 tsp) of brown sugar to taste

TOPPING

- 250g (8oz) grated mozzarella
- 80ml (⅓ cup) fresh shedded parmesan cheese
- 30ml (2 tbsp) fresh chopped basil
- 15ml (1tbsp) fresh chopped parsley

METHOD

1. In a pre-heated oven 220C (430F) place a baking tray, greased with a good non-stick cooking oil.

2. In a large mixing bowl, whisk the eggs, parsley, dried ginger, oregano and a pinch of salt and pepper. Coat each chicken filet in the mixture. Cover for at least half an hour or overnight for a deep marinated flavour.

3. Now mix the parmesan cheese and breadcrumbs in a mixing bowl. Evenly coat the chicken filets and set aside.

4. Next, heat the olive oil in a large frying pan on a medium heat and when sizzling, fry the chicken on both sides, until it has a crispy and golden look.

5. On a baking tray, place the chicken equally and top each filet with ⅓ cup of the sauce mix (below), then add a few slices of mozzarella cheese and a few tbsp of parmesan cheese, topping with the chopped basil and parsley.

SAUCE

1. Heat the olive oil in a medium sized saucepan and when up to heat, fry the optional onion or ginger for about two minutes.

2. Now add tomato puree, Oregano, basil, optional sugar and season with salt and pepper. Bring to the boil, then reduce heat and simmer for about 10 minutes. Once sauce thickens slightly, it is ready to use.

Fragrant CHICKEN PICATTA

Serves	6
Prep time	20m
Cook time	30m
Total time	50m

This tasty chicken dish is not only gorgeous, but simple to make. The succulent lemon sauce really gets your taste-buds going without being overly acidic. It is simply delightful. Serve it with crunchy roast potatoes or fragrant sticky rice.

INGREDIENTS

- 3 boneless and skinless chicken breasts fileted in halve
- 125ml (½ cup) of plain flour
- Salt and pepper to season
- 1 50mm (1") length of freshly grated ginger
- 30ml (2 tbsp) of olive oil

- ½ lemon, sliced thinly
- 60ml (¼ cup) lemon juice
- 1 cup of good quality chicken stock
- 45ml (3 tbsp) of butter
- 30ml (2 tbsp) of finely chopped parsley
- 30ml (2 tbsp) capers rinsed and drained
- Small jar of artichokes in

METHOD

1. Warm a serving dish in a Pre heated oven set to 100C (210F).

2. Take the chicken breast filets, season well with salt and pepper and then cover both sides with the flour, shaking off any excess.

3. Heat the oil in a large frying pan and fry the chicken filets in batches until golden brown on both sides (about 4m each side). Add oil as necessary. Once cooked, drain and set aside.

4. Leaving a thin layer of the oil in the frying pan, cook and stir the ginger for about 1 minute on a medium heat, taking care not to burn it.

5. Now, add the chicken stock, stirring in the lemon slices and take the mixture to the boil. Reduce to simmer, stirring intermittently until the liquid reduces by half.

6. Add the capers and lemon juice, still simmering until the liquid thickens slightly. Now add the butter and gently stir it into the sauce until it is completely dissolved. Stir in the parsley and then take of heat and set aside.

7. Place the chicken filets on serving plates, spoon the sauce over and serve while hot. Add whole parsley leaves and lemon slices to garnish.

PESCE

(FISH)

Scintillating LINGUINE WITH SHIMPS OR PRAWNS

Serves	4
Prep time	15m
Cook time	20m
Total time	35m

This is a quintessential Italian seafood pasta meal and one that always receives praise when presented to friends and family. Ideal as a quick, simple, but very tasty main course.

INGREDIENTS

- ½ kg (1 lb) pre-cooked and shelled frozen shimps or prawns
- 250g (½ lb) linguine pasta
- 750ml (3 cups) water
- 1 vegetable stock cube
- 2 finely chopped sweet tomatoes
- 50g (2oz) butter

- 1 50mm (2") clump of fresh ginger, finely chopped
- 1 optional onion - quartered
- 1 pinch of dried chili flakes
- 60ml (¼ cup) olive oil
- 20 ml (4 tsp) ouzo or Pernod

- 2.5ml (½ tsp) granulated sugar
- Salt and freshly ground pepper to season
- 5 to 6 finely chopped fresh basil leaves
- The zest of 1 lemon
- Grated parmesan

METHOD

1. Defrost the shimps.

2. In a deep saucepan add the water and 1 vegetable cube. Cover and bring to the boil, then simmer for 15 minutes. Pour the stock into a container and reserve for later.

3. Place a large frying pan over high heat. add some olive oil over the shimp, season with salt and freshly ground pepper, then when the pan gets hot add the shimp or prawns and sauté ½ minute each side. Don't cook the shimp any longer to ensure they retain a soft, succulent texture. Transfer to a plate and set aside.

4. Now, place frying pan over a high heat and add the olive oil. Add the optional onion to the pan or substitute for the ginger. Add the sugar and a pinch of chili flakes.

5. Now add 20 ml of ouzo or Pernod. Cook until the ouzo or Pernod evaporates, then add the chopped tomatoes into the pan, adding the stock and the pasta. Stir on a low to medium heat and simmer for 10 minutes taking care to gently stir thoughout

6. Once the sauce has thickened, add the butter and stir in until completely dissolved, the butter helps to thicken your sauce.

7. Remove pan from heat. Now add the shimps or prawns and the basil leaves and sprinkle over the top, grate the zest of 1 lemon and scatter on top of the pasta. Finally, add grated parmesan and stir again. Serve immediately.

8. Garnish with either whole leaf fresh parsley or basil and freshly ground pepper.

The Perfect SALMON ON MASCARPONE & BRUSCHETTA

Serves	8-10
Prep time	15m
Cook time	20m
Total time	35m

At the turn of this century I was invited to dinner at a restaurant in the beautiful Italian town of Gorgonzola, home to the famous blue cheese. I shared a starter of mascarpone cheese with smoked salmon on a crispy toasted baguette slice. It was delectable, and it inspired me to recreate this simple tasty recipe in my own kitchen. I hope you enjoy this as much as my friends and I do. Makes 30 bruschetta slices.

INGREDIENTS

- 1 baguette sliced 6-7mm (¼") thick
- 60ml (¼ cup) olive oil
- 1 50mm (2") clump of freshly grated ginger
- 300g (10oz) mascarpone cheese
- ¼ tsp sea salt
- 125ml (½ cup) sour cream
- 125ml (½ cup) lemon juice
- 60ml (¼ cup) double cream
- 1 tsp lemon zest
- 60ml (¼ cup) capers finely chopped
- 2 tbsp dried dill
- 350g (12oz) sliced smoked salmon
- Whole parsley leaves for garnish

METHOD

1. Preheat oven to 200C (400F)

2. Line a baking tray with parchment paper and lay the bruschetta slices in one layer. Lightly brush the slices with the olive oil. Bake until they are crisp and golden. Transfer the toasted slices and leave to cool. You will need 30 slices for the bruschetta,

3. Add the mascarpone and sour cream into a mixing bowl and combine until smooth. Now add the salt, lemon juice and the cream and whip until soft peaks form. Now blend in the lemon zest and capers.

TO BUILD THE BRUSCHETTA:

Smear a small amount of the mascarpone mix on to each of the toasted slices to secure the salmon. Add a slice of smoked salmon to cover the toasted slice on to the cheese paste and top the salmon with a small dollop of the cheese mix. spread the mixture out slightly and top off with the parsley. Delicious!

Crispy

CONCHIGLIONI PASTA STUFFED WITH SALMON IN TOMATO SAUCE

Serves	4
Prep time	30m
Cook time	1h 30m
Total time	2h

A firm friends and family favourite. Hugely decadent cheesy pasta shells with a basic, yet mouth-watering tomato sauce, crisply baked, with a delightful gooey filling.

INGREDIENTS

FOR THE PASTA

- 16 conchiglioni large pasta shells
- Tomato based Pomodoro sauce (recipe below)
- 1 ball of mozzarella cheese sliced
- 4 tbsp of freshly grated parmesan cheese

FOR THE FILLING

- 16 conchiglioni large pasta shells
- Tomato based Pomodoro sauce (recipe below)
- 1 ball of mozzarella cheese sliced
- 4 tbsp of freshly grated parmesan cheese

TOMATO SAUCE (SALSA DI POMODORO)

- 16 conchiglioni large pasta shells
- Tomato based Pomodoro sauce (recipe below)
- 1 ball of mozzarella cheese sliced
- 4 tbsp of freshly grated parmesan cheese

METHOD

1. Cook the pasta shells in lightly salted boiling water until al dente. Once cooked, drain ensuring that the shells are completely empty of water and set aside to cool.

2. Preheat the oven to 200C (400F)

3. For the filling, squash the ricotta with a fork, mix in the sliced mozzarella, parmesan and a pinch of salt and pepper to taste and stir well. Measure the mixture into 16 balls, encase each ball in a basil leaf and position in the cooled pasta shells.

4. For the sauce. In a large frying pan, heat the olive oil, add the ginger and gently cook on a low heat for about two minutes. Now add the basil and tomatoes, season with salt and pepper to taste and simmer gently on a low heat for about 25 minutes.

5. Meanwhile, pour a layer of the tomato sauce over the bottom of a casserole or ovenproof dish and position the filled shells on top. Now pour over the residual tomato sauce, scattering the parmesan over and top with the remaining slices of mozzarella. Cover with foil and bake for about 30-40 minutes. Now discard the foil and bake open for five minutes. Garnish with grated parmesan and a few fresh basil leaves. Serve hot immediately.

VEGETARIANO

PIZZA NEAPOLITAN

Makes 4, 12" pizzas

Prep time   20m

Prove time   1h 15m

Cook time   10m

Total time   1h 45m

Prep time   15m

Total time   15m

This is without doubt the ultimate pizza base recipe. I first made this dough about 15 years ago, after experimenting with various different recipes. It is best made with stone ground bread flour. This recipe is really simple and can be made thick or thin. I prefer thin and crispy, like the authentic Southern Italian pizza. For this recipe, I have used a base Margherita style and added a few additional toppings to make a truly scrumptious feast. It is important to make the base sauce from fresh, providing an explosion of mouth-watering flavours. Perfect for any time of the year.

INGREDIENTS

INGREDIENTS FOR DOUGH BASE

- 1 cup of warm water (about 15C)
- 2 tsp of active dried yeast
- ½ tsp of granulated sugar
- 1 tsp of table salt
- 2 tsp of olive oil
- 750ml (3 cups) of stone ground flour

INGREDIENTS FOR TOPPING

- 2 tsp of dried basil
- 250g (I cup) of pitted black olives
- A handful of sun-dried tomatoes (non-garlic)
- A pinch of fresh ground black pepper
- 250g (½ lb) of grated mozzarella cheese

- 2 tsp of dried oregano
- A handful of fresh basil leaves on each pizza
- Optional: jalapeno peppers

METHOD

BASE TOMATO SAUCE TOPPING

1. Pour the tomato passata into a mixing bowl
2. Add 1 tsp of dried oregano
3. Add pinch of salt
4. Add 2 tsp of dried basil
5. Now mix thoroughly and set aside.

TIPS: *Always gently stir and soak the dried yeast for about 5 minutes in warm water. For a crispy crust, lightly brush olive oil around the edges of the pizza base, before putting it in the oven. Always bake on the highest heat – preferably 250C (450F) to 300C (550F) or the ovens maximum temperature.*

PIZZA DOUGH BASE

1. Measure water in a measuring cup, then add the dried yeast and sugar. Stir gently then leave to stand until it is foamy and active – about 5 minutes.
2. By Hand: add salt, oil and two cups of flour into a large steel mixing bowl, stirring in the yeast mixture using a large metal spoon. Add the third cup of flour and mix and fold the dough thoroughly until it becomes difficult to mix. Then, with your hands, work the dough into a large ball. It should be slightly sticky at this stage.
3. Now spray or apply olive oil with a paper towel to the inside of a second mixing bowl and then add your pizza dough. Brush a thin film of olive oil on the top of the dough. Cover the bowl with a tight layer of plastic film. Place in a warm area of the kitchen or I prefer to leave it in the airing cupboard for between 1½ to 2 hours, dependant on ambient temperature. The dough is ready to use when it has doubled in size.
4. When the dough is ready, empty the dough onto a lightly floured work top or large wooden board. Knead the dough ball vigorously for about 5 minutes, then cut the dough into 4 equal parts, forming dough balls and leave to stand for about 15 minutes.
5. Now flatten and stretch each dough ball to your desired thickness and diameter ready for topping. Don't worry about getting the perfect circle. I prefer the look of odd shaped pizzas to give the rustic look of real homemade cooking.
6. Put two baking or pizza trays into the hot oven to preheat – 250C (450F) – 300C (550F), putting baking parchment paper on top of each tray.
7. Add the tomato base sauce adding the other ingredients. Top off with the grated mozzarella cheese and complete with draped sliced prosciutto ham. Use two teaspoons of oregano equally and lightly sprinkling over the whole of each pizza. Add olives, ham and jalapenos as required.
8. OPTIONAL: for crusty edges, lightly brush the crust with olive oil
9. Now place onto the parchment in the pre-heated baking trays and cook for between 15 – 20 minutes on 250C (450F) or for 10-15 minutes for 300C (550F).
10. The pizza is cooked once the cheese is melted and the crust is light brown.

Ultimate MUSHROOM RISOTTO

Serves	6
Prep time	15m
Cook time	50m
Total time	1h 5m

Using this simple but oh so tasty mushroom risotto recipe will quickly make this dish become a weekly staple for any household or party. Risotto is not as difficult to make to make as some make out and doesn't need a lot of ingredients. You just need the right risotto rice and determination. Ideal for a hearty winter warmer or as an entrée with a crisp green salad in the summer.

INGREDIENTS

- 2 sticks of celery
- 450g (1 lb) risotto rice
- Coarse sea salt
- One 50mm (2") clump of fresh ginger, finely grated
- Fresh ground black pepper
- 80ml (⅓ cup) white wine

- Freshly ground black pepper
- 150g (6oz) of Oyster or Shitake mushrooms, washed and sliced
- 1 sprig of tarragon plucked and chopped
- 1 tsp of butter
- 3 tbsp of dried porcini mushrooms

- 2 tbsp of freshly grated parmesan cheese
- Juice of 1 lemon
- 2 tbsp of extra virgin olive oil
- 1.5L (3 pints) of hot chicken stock

METHOD

1. Make your stock in a saucepan on a low heat and maintain a low simmer. Hydrate the porcini mushrooms by adding to a jug of some of the hot stock, enough to cover. Leave for a 5 to 10 minutes until they look completely hydrated. Take them out of the liquid and roughly chop them, putting aside the hydrating stock.

2. Now, using a large pan, heat a tbsp of olive oil and add the celery and ginger. Fry slowly without burning them for about 10-15 minutes, then turn the heat up to a medium heat and add the rice. Stir often.

3. Now mix in in the wine, constantly stirring until the liquid has soaked into the rice. Next pour the porcini hydrating liquid though a sieve into the pan to filter the residue left from the mushrooms adding the chopped porcini, salt and pepper to season and the first cup of hot stock. Turning the heat low to a simmer, keep adding cupful's of the chicken stock, constantly stirring the rice, allowing each cupful to be absorbed before adding the next cup.

4. Maintain this method until the rice is soft but not stodgy (about 30 minutes).

5. Now heat a dry frying pan on a medium heat and add the mushrooms until soft without burning. Now put them in a mixing bowl and add the freshly chopped herbs, the lemon juice and a pinch of salt. Fold all ingredients together. Take the risotto off the hob adjust the seasoning carefully. Now add the butter until it dissolves with the parmesan. Add extra stock if it looks too dry. Cover and leave the risotto to rest for about 4 minutes.

6. Serve a good portion of risotto per plate garnished with the grilled mushrooms, sprinkling freshly grated Parmesan and a few drops of extra virgin olive oil.

Authentic MUSHROOM RAVIOLETTI

Serves	4
Prep time	10m
Cook time	10m
Total time	20m

This great tasting, simple ravioletti and mushroom sauce is a delight for all. Very quick to prepare and cook, the sauce makes a superb alternative for any pasta. The combination of the mushrooms and walnuts pair so well together.

INGREDIENTS

- 350g (12oz) ravioletti or tortellini
- 30ml (2 tbsp) extra virgin olive oil
- 190ml (¾ cup) double whipping cream
- 125ml (½ cup) grated fresh Parmesan cheese
- 250g (8oz) sliced mushrooms
- 60ml (¼ cup) chopped walnuts
- Pinch of freshly ground black pepper

METHOD

1. Heat the olive oil in large frying pan over a medium heat.
2. Sauté the mushrooms and walnuts until mushrooms are a nice golden brown.
3. Now add the cream and heat, stirring often for about 6-7 minutes until just starting to thicken.
4. Next, on a medium heat and when cream stops gently bubbling, add the Parmesan cheese and pepper and stir until the sauce is smooth. Serve pasta immediately with the sauce. Garnish with a few nutty rocket lettuce leaves.

"

Everything you see, I owe to pasta!

"

--- SOPHIA LOREN

Crispy

FETTUCCINI PASTA WITH AVOCADO & PINE NUTS

Serves	6
Prep time	30m
Cook time	25m
Total time	55m

If you like avocados, I know you will love this easy to make Italian pasta classic. It is my healthy version of creamy pasta minus the cream and butter! Quick to prepare and make, it takes less than a half hour to prepare. This decadent dish has heaps of fresh basil with a touch of tangy lemon. Avocado is a super food with amazing health benefits and I am always happy to serve this dish to my family and friends.

INGREDIENTS

- 60ml (¼ cup) pine nuts
- 2 pinches of salt
- 450g (1 lb) thin spaghetti
- 2 tbsp fresh lemon juice
- 80ml (⅓ cup) fresh basil leaves chopped randomly

- 3 tbsp extra-virgin olive oil
- 1 50mm (2") clump of ginger, freshly grated
- 3 firm but ripe avocados, halved, peeled, destoned and cut into 50mm (2") cubes

- A pinch of freshly ground black pepper
- 30ml (⅛ cup) of finely grated Parmesan cheese

METHOD

1. Heat a small frying pan on a medium heat. Add the pine nuts and roll nuts in the pan randomly until they begin to brown and give off a great nutty aroma. Take off the heat and reserve for later.

2. Boil a large saucepan of salted water. Add the pasta and cook until al dente, or about a minute less than the package instruction. Save about 60ml (¼ cup) of the pasta water, draining the pasta in a colander.

3. Meanwhile, using a blender, add the olive oil, lemon juice, basil, ginger and remaining pinch of salt. Blend until well mixed. Then add the avocado and pepper and blend again until smooth and creamy.

4. Now, add the avocado mix into a large serving bowl, then add the hot pasta and mix thoroughly to combine, taking care not to damage the pasta. Add some of the reserved pasta water if needed and mix well.

5. Sprinkle with the parmesan cheese and pine nuts then serve immediately.

Life is a combination of magic and pasta.

--- FEDERICO FELLINI

Ultimate PASTA WITH MUSHROOM & CREAM SAUCE

Serves	4
Prep time	30m
Cook time	10m
Total time	40m

This is a simple yet really tasty dish that's very quick and simple to make. You can use any style of pasta for a base and before you know it, you have a main meal that everybody will delight in eating. Enjoy!

INGREDIENTS

- 2 tbsp of olive oil
- 60g (2oz) of butter
- Optional – half a mild onion, finely chopped
- Substitute for onion – 1 25mm (1") chunk of fresh ginger, finely grated
- 200ml (8fl oz) double cream
- 3 tsp of fresh parsley chopped
- 75g (3oz) of pine nuts
- 8 Portobello or shitake mushrooms roughly chopped
- Salt and freshly ground black pepper to season

METHOD

1. Melt the olive oil and butter in a frying pan and fry the onion or ginger until soft and transparent.

2. Now add the mushrooms and cook again until soft. Add a pinch of salt and pepper.

3. Cook the pasta as per pack instructions al dante, drain and reserve for later.

4. Next, add the wine, bring to the boil and then simmer on a lower heat until the amount of liquid has reduced by half.

5. Now add the cream and simmer again for 5 minutes then add the parsley and add salt and pepper again to season.

6. Finally add the pasta and fold into the sauce, serving immediately in warm bowls and garnish by scattering the pasta dish with pine nuts (optional).

"

In heaven, after antipasti. The first course will be the pasta

"

--- STEVE ALBINI

Classic
BAKED CANNELLONI WITH CHEESE & SPINACH

Serves 6

Prep time 25m

Cook time 1h

Total time 1h 25m

My preference is the beef cannelloni. But every now and then I just love to eat this juicy vegetarian alternative that really is worth all the preparation before baking. I hope you enjoy this too.

INGREDIENTS

- 450g (16oz) spinach
- 18 tubes of cannelloni
- 4 tbsp of virgin olive oil
- 1 optional onion or 25mm chunk (1") of fresh grated ginger

- 2 450g (16oz) tins of Italian chopped tomatoes
- 1 bay leaf
- ½ lemon
- Parmesan cheese

- 2 125g (4½ oz) mozzarella balls
- 250g (9oz) ricotta cheese
- A handful of fresh basil

METHOD

1. Preheat the oven to 180C (350F). Put the spinach and a drizzle of olive oil in a large pan over a low heat. Add the nutmeg, season with sea salt and black pepper, cover and leave to sweat. Help the kids to stir it occasionally until the spinach has cooked down. Place in a bowl and set to one side to cool a little.

2. Dice the optional onion or ginger. In a medium sized frying pan, heat a tbsp of olive oil and gently sweat the onion or ginger until soft.

3. Add the tomatoes and bay leaf. Drop in a few basil leaves and grate in the zest of the lemon half, then lower the heat and let it simmer gently for 25 minutes until the sauce has thickened. Add a pinch of salt and pepper.

4. Now chop the spinach on a board randomly.

5. Whisk the egg and add 2 tsps of grated Parmesan cheese. Now stir the ricotta, egg and Parmesan into the spinach. Add a pinch of salt and pepper.

6. Using a piping bag, position over a jug, fold its edges over the rim, then load in the spinach mixture. Use this to fill the mixture into the cannelloni tubes and lay them in a medium sized oven dish capable of lying the cannelloni tubes side by side in two rows.

7. Now layer the tomato sauce over the cannelloni. Add the remaining basil leaves and scatter most of them over the top of tomato sauce. lay slices of mozzarella on top, sprinkle with extra-virgin olive oil and season with salt and pepper.

8. Place in the oven and cook for 45 minutes or until the top is golden brown and the pasta tender.

9. Now, take from the oven and let it cool for a few minutes before serving, Garnish with the remaining basil leaves. Enjoy.

Magnificent PENNE PASTA WITH BASIL & PINE NUTS

Serves	4
Prep time	15m
Cook time	15m
Total time	30m

This mouth-wateringly tasty pasta dish is a firm favourite with friends and family. It is so simple and quick to make, yet so scrumptious to eat. I hope you enjoy this delectable dish as much as I do.

INGREDIENTS

- 30ml (2 tbsp) freshly ground sea salt
- 90ml (6 tbsp) olive oi
- 80ml (⅓ cup) pine nuts
- 1 50mm (2") clump of fresh ginger grated finely
- 1ml (¼) tsp. mixed or red pepper flakes
- 250ml (1 cup) fine bread crumbs (Panko bread crumbs are best)
- 250ml (1 cup) good dry white wine
- 1ml (¼ lb). grated parmesan cheese
- 165ml (⅔ cup) fresh basil leaves chopped finely
- Freshly ground black pepper to season

METHOD

1. Boil a large saucepan of salted water over high heat. Add the pasta. Cook, stirring often to prevent sticking, until the pasta is al dente according to the package instructions. Drain the pasta and reserve in saucepan and cover with lid.

2. Next, place a large frying pan over medium heat, toast the pine nuts, stirring continually until golden brown for about 2 minutes. Set aside.

3. Heat 1 tbsp of the olive oil in the pan, then add the bread crumbs, and stir until golden and then add to the the pine nuts and mix together.

4. Reduce the hob to medium and heat 1 tbsp of the olive oil in the frying pan. Now add the ginger and sauté until soft for about 1 minute. Stir in the wine and pepper flakes and bring to the boil, reducing heat immediately and then simmer until liquid is reduced by a third.

5. Finally, add the hot pasta along with the remaining 4 tbsp olive oil to the wine sauce in the pan and stir to completely coat the pasta. Now add the bread crumb and pine nut mix, the basil and cheese and stir to combine. Add salt and pepper to taste. Serve equally in pasta bowls and eat immediately.

Delicious

PASTA PENNE ALLA PUTANESCA

Serves	6
Prep time	15m
Cook time	15m
Total time	30m

For my finale in this great Italian classic's NO GARLIC volume, a meal that is large on flavour and super quick on time. This amazingly simple Southern Italian dish features a host of tongue tingling ingredients. The whole recipe can be prepared and made in less time than it takes to cook the pasta itself and is ideal for a simple weekday evening meal.

INGREDIENTS

- 500g (16oz) Penne pasta
- 15ml (1 tbsp) extra-virgin olive oil
- 2 Whole anchovies
- 30g (2 tbsp) Salted capers
- 256g (1 cup) black olives
- 1 25mm (1") clump of fresh ginger, finely grated
- 5g (1 tsp) chopped parsley
- 360g (1½ cups) Can of chopped Italian tomatoes
- Sea salt and freshly ground black pepper to season

METHOD

1. Boil a large saucepan of salted water. Add the penne pasta to the pan, stir, and cook until al dente, about 1 minute less than the pack instructions.

2. Meanwhile, for the sauce, heat the oil in a frying pan over a low heat.

3. Now, wash the anchovies and the capers in cold water to remove the salt, then soak in a bowl of water for about 10 minutes.

4. Remove the stones from the olives, then halve the anchovies by removing the backbone. Add the anchovies, capers, ginger, parsley, and olives to the frying pan, and cook until the anchovies are broken up and the ginger is slightly browned.

5. Add the chopped tomatoes to the frying pan and simmer sauce for 2 to 3 minutes. Check for seasoning and add pepper to taste.

6. Add the puttanesca sauce into the saucepan of pasta and cook over a low heat, gently folding the pasta into the sauce for 1 to 2 minutes allowing it to fuse with the sauce. Finally transfer to a serving dish or bowl, then top with finely chopped parsley and serve immediately.

THE NO GARLIC COOKBOOK
Titles in the Series

Printed in Great Britain
by Amazon

57761111R00057